Pearson Baccalaureate PYP Readers

Sydney the Kangaroo

Malachy Doyle
Illustrated by Delphine Thomas

Sydney was born in the red dust of the Australian bush. As soon as he was born, he climbed up his mother's fur towards her pouch and climbed inside. He felt safe and warm in there.

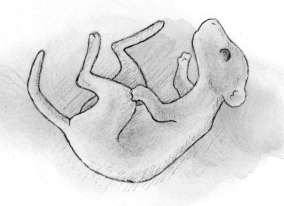

Sydney stayed in
his mother's pouch
for many months.

He grew bigger, and
his back legs and tail grew
longer. Soft grey fur grew
all over him. His ears
became pointed, just like
his mother's.

Then, one day, Sydney was big enough to peep
out of the pouch. The bright light made him
blink as he felt the warm sun for the first time.
A gentle breeze tickled his face.

Sydney watched his mother bend down
to eat grass. Sydney tried to eat some, too.
The next thing he knew, he was rolling on the
ground and his mother was looking down at him.

He had tumbled out of her pouch!

As Sydney got older, he spent more and more time out of the pouch. He learned to hop and jump, springing into the air with his strong back legs.

"Well done, Sydney," said his mother, proudly. "You will grow up to be a big, strong kangaroo."

One warm afternoon, Sydney and his mother
went looking for some fresh, tasty grass to eat.
Suddenly his mother's nose twitched.

"Dingoes!" she hissed, sniffing the air.
Sydney looked up, frightened.

In the distance he could see a band of wild
dogs – dingoes! They looked fierce and hungry.
Sydney dived into his mother's pouch. He trembled
when he heard the dogs begin to howl.

Sydney's mother stood still. She hoped the hungry dingoes would not see or smell her. But they came closer and closer, until she knew she had to get away.

"Hold tight," she whispered to Sydney.
Then, with great flying leaps, she bounded away
through the bushes. Sydney was afraid he might
fall out, but his mother had tightened her
pouch, so he was safe.

Sydney peeped out and saw the dingoes
close behind, howling and snarling.
  "Run, Mother, run!" he cried.

Sydney's mother ran as fast as she could but
she soon grew tired. She knew she would have
to stand and fight.

The dingoes closed in on her, trying to bite.
She kicked them and scratched them, and
kept them away from little Sydney.

Just then, a great buck kangaroo appeared.
He was a giant of a kangaroo, with a creamy
chest and a broad, red back. He thumped his
tail on the ground when he saw the dingoes,
and then he leaped at them. The dingoes were
so frightened of the great buck that they ran away.

Then the great buck smiled at Sydney and
bounded off into the haze of the late afternoon.

In the cool of the evening, Sydney curled up in his mother's pouch, safe again.

"Soon I'll be too big for your pouch, Mother," said Sydney.

"Yes, soon you'll be a big, strong kangaroo, just like the great buck," replied his mother.

Sydney closed his eyes, went to sleep, and dreamed about fighting dingoes.